51 Portuguese Idioms
Speak Like a Brazilian

Written by

Luciana Lage
&
Renata Barboza-Murray

51 Portuguese Idioms: Speak Like a Brazilian
by Luciana Lage & Renata Barboza-Murray

Published by Street Smart Brazil Publishing
Copyright © Luciana Lage and Renata Barboza-Murray, 2011

ISBN-13: 978-1-939405-00-5
ISBN 10: 1-939405-00-9

Credits:
Reviewed by: Adam Lee
Cover Design by: Carl Spanoghe

To our family and students,
who inspire and motivate us daily.

To Carl Spanoghe,
for his invaluable contributions
to Street Smart Brazil.

Contents

Foreword

While editing 51 Portuguese Idioms, I came across roughly 15 phrases that I hadn't seen before. It's not as if I just started learning Portuguese last year or anything, because in reality, I've been doing it for close to a decade. The fact that 51 Portuguese Idioms goes beyond all that I have seen and heard while dealing with aspects of Brazilian culture and the Portuguese language on a daily basis is no small feat. It just goes to show how varied Brazilian Portuguese really is and why, in many aspects, it is the gift that keeps on giving.

Another important aspect of learning colloquial expressions is that they take you beyond the typical exercises of verbal conjugations and syntax memorization. Learning and understanding everyday phrases in Portuguese allows the student to take their head out of the traditional textbooks and gain insight into Brazilian culture.

It is my hope that you will enjoy and learn from this book as much as I did and come to understand how intertwined culture and language really are.

Adam Lee
Editor of Eyes On Brazil
EyesOnBrazil.com

Introduction

With Brazil's economy on the rise and the country's popularity growing among leisure travelers and scholars of different fields, the demand for learning Brazilian Portuguese is higher than ever before. Add to that the World Cup (2014) and the Olympics (2016) coming to Brazil and there is no better time to learn Brazilian Portuguese and to get to know Brazilian culture.

Through our more than ten years of teaching Portuguese as a foreign language, we have taught students from all walks of life, different cultural backgrounds, and varying previous experience with the language. One thing seemed to unite all the students: The challenge to bridge the gap between the Portuguese they learned in textbooks and the Portuguese that they were exposed to in real-life interactions with Brazilians.

Our aim is to help you cross that bridge and speak like a Brazilian: *51 Portuguese Idioms* brings you the Portuguese that you won't learn in traditional books or classes. With this book you will learn idiomatic expressions, modern day slang, and popular sayings that are pervasive in everyday real-life communication.

Join us to learn Street Smart Brazilian Portuguese in a fun and effective way:

✓ Follow seven Brazilian characters as they go about their daily lives

✓ Learn colloquial expressions in the context of real-life situations that any of us might face

✓ Get to know more about Brazil through our Cultural Notes

✓ Improve your grammar with pointers to our blog posts and video lessons

✓ Build vocabulary that is current and relevant to personal and professional relationships

How this Book is Presented

The book presents 51 Brazilian Portuguese Street Smart words & expressions in the context of 102 everyday situations. Each word and expression is presented in two different situations that mirror daily interactions in modern day Brazil.

The 102 situations are presented in English, so you can focus your attention completely on the Street Smart vocabulary that you are learning. The sentences that contain the 51 colloquial words and expressions are presented in Portuguese followed by their English translation. Through these Portuguese/English examples you will build vocabulary beyond the colloquial expressions that are the primary goal of this book.

Who Will Benefit from this Book

Students of all levels of language ability will benefit from learning Brazilian Portuguese Street Smart vocabulary to enhance their ability to communicate effectively in any situation.

Authors' Note

Though the authors and the publisher have used their best efforts in preparing this book, they make no representations or warranties with respect to accuracy or completeness of the contents of this book, and specifically disclaim any implied warranties or merchantability or fitness for a particular purpose. The translations offered here are not literal. The expressions and vocabulary contained herein may not be suitable for your situation. Neither the authors nor the editor or the publisher shall be liable for any damages.

Meet Your Travel Companions

Aqui estão seus companheiros de viagem para esta jornada de português coloquial.

Here are your travel mates for this colloquial Portuguese journey.

Ana é brasileira e mora em São Paulo. Ela é atriz. Seu sonho é trabalhar internacionalmente.

Ana is Brazilian and lives in São Paulo. She is an actress. Her dream is to work internationally.

Fernando é o namorado de Ana. Ele trabalha em uma agência de publicidade em São Paulo.

Fernando is Ana's boyfriend. He works in an advertising agency in São Paulo.

Artur é amigo de Fernando e é casado com Cibele. Ele trabalha em uma grande empresa brasileira.

Artur is friends with Fernando and is married to Cibele. He works for a large Brazilian company.

Cibele é de Salvador. Há oito anos ela mora em São Paulo. Cibele é dona de uma butique.

Cibele is from Salvador. She has been living in São Paulo for eight years. Cibele owns a boutique.

Marcelo joga futebol desde os cinco anos de idade. Ele é um excelente goleiro.

Marcelo has been playing soccer since he was five years old. He is an excellent goalkeeper.

Seu Bernardo e Dona Antonieta são os pais de Marcelo. Eles não perdem um jogo do filho.

Mr. Bernando and Mrs. Antonieta are Marcelo's parents. They don't miss any of their son's games.

Gabriela é estudante universitária e trabalha na butique de Cibele. Seus amigos a chamam de Gabi.

Gabriela is a college student and works at Cibele's boutique. Her friends call her Gabi.

1. Abrir mão (de)

Situation 1:

Fernando is upset. His girlfriend Ana is going to work in Los Angeles and wants him to go with her. Fernando has a good job, family and friends in São Paulo. He talks to a friend and says:

> *"Não sei o que fazer. Quero morar com Ana, mas não quero <u>abrir mão</u> da minha vida em São Paulo."*

> **Translation:** I don't know what to do. I want to live with Ana, but I don't want to give up my life in São Paulo.

 **Learn how to use the Possessive Pronouns.** Check out our blog post: *Possessive Pronouns and Adjectives: Own Them Now!* http://goo.gl/wFdAF

Situation 2:

Artur has a big day at work today. He is about to close a very important deal. Before he leaves to the office his wife wishes him luck. Artur says:

> *"Serei assertivo na conversa de hoje. Quero o contrato, mas não vou <u>abrir mão</u> de algumas condições que considero importantes."*

Translation: I will be assertive in today's conversation. I want the contract, but I will not give up on some conditions that I consider important.

2. Acertar em cheio

Situation 1:

Artur and Cibele are watching a soccer game on TV. Artur says:

"Acho que o jogo vai ser 1 a 0."

Translation: I think the game will be 1-0.

At the end of the game, the score is 1-0. Cibele says:

"Você acertou em cheio!"

Translation: You got it right!

Situation 2:

Artur comes home from work with a broad smile. His wife asks him if he finally got the promotion he always wanted. He answers:

"Acertou em cheio!

Translation: You got it right!

3. Agarrar (uma oportunidade/ chance) com unhas e dentes

Situation 1:

Ana is an actress. She has been invited to live in Los Angeles and act in a Hollywood movie. She talks to her friend, Cibele:

> Cibele: *Você vai mesmo mudar para L.A.?*
>
> Ana: *Vou sim, tenho que <u>agarrar esta chance com unhas e dentes</u>.*

Translation:

> Cibele: Are you really moving to L.A.?
>
> Ana: Yes, I am. I have to make the most out of this opportunity.

Situation 2:

Marcelo is a good goalkeeper but so far he has always been a bench player. When he was invited to play as a starter for another team, he didn't think twice. He knew he had to <u>*agarrar esta oportunidade com unhas e dentes*</u> (make the most out of this opportunity) to show his talent to the world.

4. Antes tarde do que nunca

Situation 1:

Artur was invited for his best friend's birthday dinner that night. He got to the restaurant at the end of dinner because he had to stay at the office until 10 pm. When his friends joke about that night, Artur says:

"*Antes tarde do que nunca!*"

Translation: Better late than never!

Situation 2:

Ana is always late to meet with her friends. When she arrives she usually says:

"*Cheguei, pessoal! Antes tarde do que nunca!*"

Translation: I'm here, folks! Better late than never!

5. Bagaço/Estar um bagaço

Situation 1:

Ana is exhausted after two days packing her books, clothes, and furniture. Fernando wants to go out for dinner but she says:

> *"Prefiro ficar em casa. Estou um bagaço."*

> **Translation:** I'd rather stay home. I'm a wreck.

Situation 2:

Marcelo has an important game coming up. He and his team have been practicing harder than usual. *Todos os jogadores estão se sentindo um bagaço.* (All the players are feeling exhausted.)

6. O bicho vai pegar

Situation 1:

Artur asks Marcelo if he is ready for the big game. Marcelo answers:

> *"Esse vai ser um jogo difícil. O bicho vai pegar."*

> **Translation:** This is going to be a difficult game. Things will get ugly.

Situation 2:

Ana and Fernando are going to Salvador for Carnival. They are very excited about it. Ana says:

> *"A gente vai se divertir tanto lá! O bicho vai pegar."*

> **Translation:** We are going to have so much fun there! It's going to be awesome.

Cultural Note:
As you can see, the expression "*o bicho vai pegar*" has a negative and a positive meaning. It depends on the context.

Learn how to use tanto correctly. Check out our video lesson on *How to Use Tão and Tanto Correctly*: http://goo.gl/2Hqog

Learn how to use *a gente*. Watch our video lesson on *"A Gente" – Make Your Portuguese Even Smarter*: http://goo.gl/kfxBl

7. Bater perna (por/em)

Situation 1:

Cibele's mother lives in Salvador. Cibele is writing an e-mail to her mother:

> *"Oi mãe, tudo bem? Hoje passei o dia <u>batendo perna</u> pela Rua 25 de Março e comprei uma lembrancinha para você. Saudades."*

> **Translation:** Hi mom, how are you? I spent the day strolling around 25 de Março Street and I bought a souvenir for you. I miss you.

Cultural Note:
Rua 25 de Março is actually more than just one street. It is an area near downtown São Paulo known for its very active commerce. You can pretty much find everything in the Rua 25 de Março shops, and prices are usually lower than anywhere else. During the holiday season, large crowds stroll the streets of 25 de Março looking for good deals.

Situation 2:

Ana is getting ready to move to Los Angeles. Today she had several errands to run and walked a lot to get everything done. When Fernando asked about her day, her answer was:

"Bati perna o dia todo para resolver um monte de coisas."

Translation: I walked around all day and ran several errands.

8. Botar pra quebrar

Situation 1:

Artur and Cibele are planning a farewell party for Ana. They want it to be the best party ever. It was. At the end of the party, Ana says:

> *"Vocês <u>botaram pra quebrar</u>. A festa foi ótima! Valeu!"*

Translation: You guys rocked! The party was awesome! Thanks!

Street Smart Portuguese:
Pra is a short form of the preposition "para". It is widely used in spoken Brazilian Portuguese and in very colloquial written communication such as personal emails.

Situation 2:

Fernando and his assistant are working together on a documentary about Brazilian rock and roll. They want to do their best. Fernando:

> *"Vamos <u>botar pra quebrar</u>! Esse documentário vai ser um sucesso!"*

> **Translation**: Let's give it all we got! This documentary is going to be a success.

9. Bugiganga

Situation 1:

Ana is packing up to move to L.A. After sorting out the objects in her bedroom she realizes she has a lot of junk.

> *"Caramba, quanta <u>bugiganga</u>!"*
>
> **Translation:** Gosh, so much junk!

Situation 2:

Seu Bernardo collects objects that he finds on the streets. His wife gets really upset when he comes home with a new "find":

> *"Mais uma <u>bugiganga</u> para sua coleção?"*
>
> **Translation:** More junk for your collection?

10. Cadê?

Situation 1:

Artur is in a hurry to go to work, but he cannot find his car keys. He asks Cibele:

> *"Amor, <u>cadê</u> a chave do meu carro? Você pegou?"*

> **Translation:** Sweetie, where are my car keys? Did you take them?

Situation 2:

When Artur is on his way to work, one of his colleagues calls him on his cell phone:

> *"<u>Cadê</u> você? Você vai chegar na hora para a reunião?"*

> **Translation:** Where are you? Are you going to get here on time for the meeting?

11. Cochilo/ Tirar um cochilo

Situation 1:

Seu Bernardo likes to take a nap in the afternoon. When his friends call him to go out, he says:

> *"Só saio depois do meu cochilo."*

> **Translation:** I only go out after my nap.

Situation 2:

Dona Antonieta does not like to take naps during the day:

> *"Se eu tirar um cochilo, não consigo dormir à noite."*

> **Translation:** If I take a nap, I cannot sleep at night.

12. Colocar o papo em dia

Situation 1:

Cibele hasn't seen Marcelo for a while because he has been busy practicing for the soccer championship. She calls him:

> *"Oi Marcelo, como vai a vida? Precisamos <u>colocar o papo em dia</u>."*

> **Translation:** Hi Marcelo, how's life? We need to catch up.

Situation 2:

Ana and Cibele had a girls' night out and could finally catch up. The next day, Cibele texts Ana:

> *"Ontem à noite foi ótimo! Finalmente conseguimos <u>colocar o papo em dia</u>."*

> **Translation:** Last night was great! We were finally able to catch up!

13. Dar branco

Situation 1:

Fernando is taking English lessons. Last night, he had an exam, but didn't do a good job. He told his girlfriend:

> *"<u>Deu um branco</u>. Esqueci quase tudo que tinha estudado."*

> **Translation:** I drew a blank. I forgot almost everything that I had studied.

Situation 2:

When a friend asked Seu Bernardo the date of his wedding, he said:

> *"Não lembro. <u>Deu branco</u>."*

> **Translation:** I can't rememeber. I drew a blank.

14. Dar galho

Situation 1:

Seu Bernardo and Dona Antonieta are on their way to Marcelo's game when their car breaks down. They call Marcelo and say:

> *"Não vamos chegar aí a tempo. <u>Deu um galho</u> no motor."*

> **Translation:** We won't get there on time. There's a problem with the engine.

Situation 2:

Artur is in the middle of an important report when his computer shuts down. He will have to work late to finish it. Artur calls Cibele:

> *"Vou chegar mais tarde. <u>Deu um galho</u> no computador."*

> **Translation:** I'm going to be late. There is a problem with my computer.

15. Dar um pulo

Situation 1:

Marcelo has been very busy practicing for the soccer championship. He calls his mother, Dona Antonieta:

> *"Oi mãe, tudo bem? Posso <u>dar um pulo</u> aí no fim de semana?"*

> **Translation:** Hi mom, how are you? Can I stop by over the weekend?

Situation 2:

Artur has a cold and stays home. Cibele comes from work with a treat for him:

Cibele: *<u>Dei um pulo</u> na padaria e trouxe uns brigadeiros pra você.*

Translation:

Cibele: I stopped by the bakery and brought you some brigadeiros.

Brigadeiro: Photo by Rod Senna, Flickr, Creative Commons license http://goo.gl/kY43U

27

Cultural Note:
Brigadeiro is one of Brazil's most popular treats. It is a soft chocolate sweet made with condensed milk and cocoa. Every Brazilian knows *brigadeiro*, and everyone who tries it likes it.

Make your own *brigadeiros*; it is easy. Watch our video for a delicious step-by-step recipe and learn *How to Make Brigadeiro*: http://goo.gl/01HNP

16. De tirar o fôlego

Situation 1:

Ana is ready to go out. When Fernando sees her, he says:

"Você está <u>de tirar o fôlego</u>!"

Translation: You are stunning!

Situation 2:

Ana and Fernando went to Rio de Janeiro. They are showing the pictures they took at Christ the Redeemer to their friends.

Ana: *A vista de lá de cima é <u>de tirar o fôlego</u>.*

Translation:

Ana: The view from up there is breathtaking.

17. Dia sim, dia não

Situation 1:

Cibele is very athletic. She goes to the gym *dia sim, dia não* (every other day).

Situation 2:

Cibele is concerned about falling sales and is trying to cut costs:

> *"Não preciso de serviços de limpeza todos os dias da semana. Vou reduzir o serviço para dia sim, dia não."*

Translation: I don't need cleaning services every day of the week. I will reduce it to every other day.

18. Encher a cara

Situation 1:

Last night, Artur went out with a few friends and had too much to drink. Today he has a hangover. His co-worker says:

> *"Artur tá de ressaca. Acho que ele <u>encheu a cara</u> ontem."*

> **Translation:** Artur has a hangover. I think he drank like a fish yesterday.

Street Smart Portuguese:
Tá is a short form of the verb *estar* conjugated: *Você (ele, ela) está = Você (ele, ela) tá.* It is widely used in informal spoken and written Brazilian Portuguese, such as personal emails and text messages. You are also going to hear other short versions of *estar* with different tenses and conjugations. E.g.: *Eu tô = Eu estou; Ele tava = Ele estava.*

Situation 2:

Seu Bernardo likes to go out with friends for a couple of beers every other weekend. Every time he does that, his wife warns him:

"Não vá <u>encher a cara</u>, por favor!"

Translation: Don't go drinking like a fish, please!

19. Fazer as malas

Situation 1:

Ana is very excited about moving to the U.S. *Ela já começou a <u>fazer as malas</u>.* (She has already started packing.)

Situation 2:

Dona Antonieta *está <u>fazendo as malas</u>* (is packing) to go on a tour around Northeastern Brazil with Seu Bernardo.

20. Fazer as pazes

Situation 1:

Most couples say that the best part of having an argument is *fazer as pazes* (making amends).

Situation 2:

Marcelo and Fernando used to be good friends. They had a big argument and spent a few years without speaking to each other. Ana is glad because *eles fizeram as pazes* (they made amends).

 Learn how to use the Infinitive. Check out our video lesson on *The Infinitive as the Subject:* http://goo.gl/md4Xb

21. Derreter de calor

Situation 1:

São Paulo is known as the Terra da Garoa and the weather is usually damp. Today it is exceptionally hot. Marcelo is practicing for the soccer game and *está <u>derretendo de calor</u>* (is sweating like a pig).

Cultural Note:

Terra da Garoa literally means "Land of the drizzling rain". When in São Paulo, you can hear the *paulistanos* – those who are from the city of São Paulo – saying that their city can have all four seasons in the same day. It is common to see those who live in the city carrying their winter clothes and their umbrella around in the middle of the summer.

Situation 2:

In Teresina, capital of Piauí, in the Northeast of Brazil, the temperature reaches the 90's (F) almost every day. Seu Bernardo and Dona Antonieta were walking around the city and went back to the hotel for a shower because *eles estavam derretendo de calor* (they were sweating like pigs).

Cultural Note:
Teresina is the only capital in the Brazilian Northeast that is not located on the coast of the Atlantic Ocean.

22. Que surpresa!

Situation 1:

It's Marcelo's day off. He misses his friend Cibele, and passes by her boutique to say "hi". When Cibele sees him, she says:

"Marcelo, que surpresa!"

Translation: Marcelo, what a surprise!

Situation 2:

Marcelo calls his parents who are in Teresina, Piauí.

Marcelo: *Oi mãe, tudo bem por aí?*

Dona Antonieta: *Marcelo, meu filho, que surpresa boa! Aqui tá tudo ótimo!*

Translation:

Marcelo: Hi mom, is everything okay over there?

Dona Antonieta: Marcelo, my son, what a nice surprise! Everything's fine here!

23. Dar mole

Situation 1:

Most major cities in Brazil have intense traffic and not many bike lanes. If you want to commute by bike in the city, you need to be very careful. *Você não pode <u>dar mole</u>.* (You cannot let your guard down.)

Situation 2:

Artur and Marcelo are in a bar.

Artur: *Marcelo, aquela mulher tá <u>dando mole</u> pra você.*

Marcelo: *Nem notei!*

Translation:

Artur: Marcelo, that woman seems interested in you.

Marcelo: I didn't even notice!

24. Que tal?

Situation 1:

Ana wants to go to the movies tonight. She calls Fernando:

Ana: *Oi amor, <u>que tal</u> um cineminha hoje à noite?*

Fernando: *Claro, te pego às 8.*

Translation:

Ana: Hi sweetie, how about a lil' movie tonight?

Fernando: Sure, I will pick you up at 8.

Situation 2:

Cibele: *Ana, vamos para a academia hoje à noite?*

Ana: *Não posso, vou sair com o Fernando. <u>Que tal</u> amanhã?*

Translation:

Cibele: Ana, let's go the gym tonight.

Ana: I can't. I'm going out with Fernando. How about tomorrow?

25. Empanturrar-se de

Situation 1:

Seu Bernardo and Dona Antonieta are in Salvador, Bahia. They tried *acarajé* for the first time. Seu Bernardo liked it a lot and <u>*empanturrou-se de*</u> *acarajé* (he got stuffed with acarajé).

Photo: *Acarajé*

Cultural Note:
Acarajé is a traditional dish from Bahia. It is made with black-eyed peas, deep fried in *dendê* oil (palm oil), and stuffed with shrimps.

Situation 2:

Gabriela went to a friend's barbecue and ate too much. The next morning she tells Cibele:

> *"Ontem eu me <u>empanturrei de</u> tanta carne.*

> **Translation:** Yesterday I stuffed myself with so much steak.

26. Frio na barriga

Situation 1:

Dona Antonieta was kind of nervous. It was her first time on a plane. *Ela sentiu um frio na barriga* (she felt butterflies in her stomach) during take-off.

Situation 2:

Cibele: *Gabi, você vai sair com o Marcelo de novo?*

Gabi: *Vou sim. Só de pensar dá um frio na barriga!*

Translation:

Cibele: Gabi, are you going out with Marcelo again?

Gabi: Yes, I am. Just thinking about it gives me butterflies in my stomach!

27. Enxaqueca

Situation 1:

Dona Antonieta is not feeling well after the long drive from Salvador (capital of the state of Bahia) to Maceió (capital of the state of Alagoas). *Ela está com enxaqueca* (she has a migraine).

Situation 2:

Cibele is not going to work today. She calls Gabi:

> *"Gabi, vou ficar em casa hoje. Tô com uma enxaqueca terrível."*

Translation: Gabi, I'm staying home today. I have a terrible migraine.

28. Um dia daqueles

Situation 1:

During breakfast, Fernando comments:

> *"Hoje vai ser <u>um dia daqueles</u>: tenho uma reunião importantíssima com um novo cliente e outra com meu chefe. Além disso, preciso terminar dois relatórios antes das 5h."*

Translation: Today is going to be one of those days: I have a meeting with a new client and another one with my boss. Besides, I need to finish two reports before 5pm.

Situation 2:

Cibele had to run several errands today. It was raining, she did not have her umbrella, and traffic was close to impossible. Later at home she told Artur:

> *"Ai, hoje foi <u>um dia daqueles</u>!"*

Translation: Ugh, today was one of those days!

29. Verde de fome

Situation 1:

After spending all day on a boat along the seashore of Maragogi beach, Alagoas, Seu Bernardo goes to a nearby seafood restaurant and orders:

"Uma moqueca, por favor. Tô <u>verde de fome.</u>"

Translation: A moqueca, please. I'm starving.

Photo: *Moqueca*

Cultural Note:
Moqueca is a traditional Brazilian seafood stew. You will find it in the best restaurants around the country.

Situation 2:

Gabi is watching Marcelo's soccer practice. It's almost 1pm and *ela está <u>verde de fome</u>* (she is starving).

30. Matar a saudade

Situation 1:

Cibele is planning a trip to Salvador, her hometown. She can't wait to see her entire family and eat her favorite food: acarajé.

> *"Vou <u>matar a saudade</u> de tudo e de todos."*

> **Translation:** I'm finally going to be reunited with everything and everyone.

Cultural Note:
Saudade (feminine noun) is the Portuguese word to express the deep feeling of missing something or someone. In 2004, the BBC published a study saying that *saudade* was the 7th most difficult to translate word in the world.

Situation 2:

Dona Antonieta misses Marcelo and calls him:

Dona Antonieta: *Oi filho, estou ligando pra dizer que está tudo bem e pra <u>matar a saudade</u>.*

Translation:

Dona Antonieta: Hi son, I'm calling to say that everything is alright and to get caught up because I miss you.

31. Pé quente

Situation 1:

Marcelo invited Gabi to watch his first soccer game with the new team. The weather forecast predicted a storm. After the game:

Gabi: *Marcelo, parabéns! Que jogão!*

Marcelo: *Obrigado, o time foi bem em campo. E estou feliz porque não choveu. Você é pé quente.*

Translation:

Gabi: Marcelo, congratulations! What a game!

Marcelo: Thanks, the team did well. And I am happy that it did not rain. You are lucky.

Situation 2:

Cibele won the lottery twice. All her friends say she is *pé quente* (lucky).

32. Quem me dera

Situation 1:

Ana is talking with Cibele about her upcoming move to Los Angeles. She suggests that Cibele spends a few months there with her. Cibele answers:

"Quem me dera poder tirar umas longas férias. Não posso ficar longe da loja por mais de uma semana."

Translation: I wish I could take a long vacation. I can't stay away from the store for more than a week.

Situation 2:

Cibele: *Gabi, você e o Marcelo estão mesmo namorando?*

Gabi: *Ah, quem me dera! A gente tá só ficando.*

Translation:

Cibele: Gabi, are you and Marcelo really dating?

Gabi: Oh, I wish! We are just having a fling.

33. Balada

Situation 1:

Fernando: *O que vocês vão fazer amanhã à noite?*

Artur: V*amos pra <u>balada</u> do Brasil Pub.*

Translation:

Fernando: What are you guys doing tomorrow night?

Artur: We are going out to dance at Brasil Pub.

Photo: *Balada*

Situation 2:

Gabi and Marcelo are going out to dance. They run into Artur and Cibele at the club.

Gabi: *Oba, a <u>balada</u> ficou ainda melhor com a Cibele e o Artur aqui!*

Translation:

Gabi: Yay, the party just got even better with Cibele and Artur here!

Cultural Note:
Balada (feminine noun) is a modern word to describe a party, usually in a nightclub, where you go with friends to drink, dance, flirt, and meet new people.

34. A noite é uma criança

Situation 1:

Artur worked all day. It's 1am, he is at the dance club with Cibele, Gabi, and Marcelo, but he is very tired.

Artur: *Gente, acho que está na hora de irmos.*

Marcelo: *Fica mais um pouco, Artur. <u>A noite é uma criança</u>.*

Translation:

Artur: Folks, I think it's time to go.

Marcelo: Stay a little more, Artur. The night is still young.

Situation 2:

In Brazil, nightclubs are usually open from 11pm – 5am.

Marcelo: *Gabi, agora tá na hora de ir. Já são mais de 2h da manhã.*

Gabi: *Marcelo, você acabou de dizer que <u>a noite é uma criança</u>. Vamos ficar mais uma hora, tá bom?*

Translation:

Marcelo: Gabi, now it's time to go. It's already past 2am.

Gabi: Marcelo, you just said the night had just begun. Let's stay for one more hour, okay?

35. Ser /Estar Massa

Situation 1:

Fernando: *E aí, Artur, como foi a balada de ontem?*

Artur: <u>*Foi massa*</u>. *Você devia ter ido com a gente.*

Translation:

Fernando: So, how was the party last night?

Artur: It was awesome. You should have come with us.

Situation 2:

Ana:	*Cibele, você pode me dar uma carona para a academia?*
Cibele:	*Claro, te pego em meia hora.*
Ana:	*<u>Tá massa</u>, valeu!*

Translation:

Ana:	Cibele, can you give me a ride to the gym?
Cibele:	Sure. I will pick you up in half an hour.
Ana:	Awesome, thanks!

36. Dar de cara com

Situation 1:

Dona Antonieta had a great surprise. While she was at the beach in Salvador, *ela deu de cara com seu ator de novelas preferido* (she ran into her favorite soap opera actor).

Situation 2:

Cibele:	*Ana, adivinha o que aconteceu ontem.*
Ana:	*O quê?*
Cibele:	*Eu estava saindo da butique e dei de cara com um ex-namorado meu.*

Translation:

Cibele:	Ana, guess what happened yesterday.
Ana:	What?
Cibele:	I was just leaving the boutique and ran into an ex-boyfriend.

37. Moleza

Situation 1:

Gabi is getting a Bachelor's in Business. She just had an exam and is talking to a classmate:

> *"Pensei que a prova ia ser <u>moleza</u>, mas foi bem difícil."*

> **Translation:** I thought the exam would be a piece of cake, but it was pretty hard.

Situation 2:

Marcelo's soccer team won a game by 3-0. His parents watched it on TV. After the game they called Marcelo:

Seu Bernardo: *Filho, o jogo foi <u>moleza</u>, hein?*

Marcelo: *Pois é, não precisei defender nenhum chute perigoso.*

Translation:

Seu Bernardo: Son, the game was easy, huh?

Marcelo: You're right; I didn't need to defend any risky kick.

38. Tirar de letra

Situation 1:

Artur is excited about participating in a conference in Chicago, IL. It's his first time abroad and he is not sure whether he will be able to understand and talk to people in English. He is sharing his concerns with Cibele:

Artur: *Não sei se vou entender tudo o que os americanos disserem.*

Cibele: *Ah, que nada. Você vai <u>tirar isso de letra</u>.*

Artur: *Espero que sim!*

Translation:

Artur: I don't know if I will understand everything the Americans say.

Cibele: Oh, no worries. You are going to sail through the experience.

Artur: I hope so!

Situation 2:

Fernando had a very important meeting with some investors for his new project. At the end of the meeting, he talks to his secretary:

> Fernando: *Puxa, que reunião! Eles fizeram muitas perguntas sobre toda a parte financeira do projeto. Agora, vamos aguardar pela aprovação deles.*

> Secretária: *Não se preocupe. O senhor tirou de letra, Seu Fernando. Parabéns!*

Translation:

> Fernando: Man, what a meeting! They asked a lot of questions about the project's finances. Now let's wait for their approval.

> Secretary: Don't worry. You sailed through the meeting, Mr. Fernando. Congratulations!

39. Pregar o olho

Situation 1:

Gabi's finals at school are this week. She has 3 exams and one project to finish. For two nights, *ela não pregou os olhos estudando para as provas finais* (she did not shut her eyes while studying for the finals).

Situation 2:

Fernando hasn't decided if he is going to Los Angeles with Ana or not. During the day he doesn't think about it, but at night, *ele não consegue pregar os olhos pensando no seu futuro* (he can barely sleep thinking about his future).

40. Pra burro

Situation 1:

Seu Bernardo and Dona Antonieta are stuck in the hotel. *Tá chovendo pra burro em São Luís, Maranhão.* (It's raining cats and dogs in São Luís, Maranhão.)

De São Paulo, Do Brasil – Learn How to Say It Right. Learn how to use the correct preposition and article with countries, states, and cities
http://goo.gl/9eCrz

Situation 2:

Artur and Cibele are planning a weekend getaway. *Artur trabalhou pra burro durante a semana e precisa relaxar.* (Artur worked a lot during the week and needs to relax.)

41. Mudar de ideia

Situation 1:

Dona Antonieta was planning to go for a walk at the beach, but because of the rain *ela mudou de ideia* (she changed her mind).

Situation 2:

Fernando is worried. It's been three days and he hasn't received an answer from the investors on his project. He thinks to himself: *Espero que eles não mudem de ideia.* (I hope they don't change their mind.)

42. Ficar

Situation 1:

Ana:	*A Gabi e o Marcelo estão namorando?*
Cibele:	*Não tenho certeza. Segundo ela, eles <u>estão apenas ficando</u>.*

Translation:

Ana:	Are Gabi and Marcelo dating?
Cibele:	I'm not sure. According to her, they're just having a fling.

Situation 2:

Ana and Fernando are looking at some old pictures.

Ana: *Olha só, a foto do casamento da Cibele e do Artur! Nós dois estamos na foto, mas nem namorávamos ainda.*

Fernando: *É verdade. Mas nesse dia nós <u>ficamos</u>.*

Translation:

Ana: Look, a picture from Cibele and Artur's wedding! We are both in the picture but we weren't even dating yet.

Fernando: That's true, but on that day we got together.

43. Falar pelos cotovelos

Situation 1:

Dona Antonieta loves a good conversation. Seu Bernardo is always teasing her: *A Antonieta <u>fala pelos cotovelos</u>.* (Antonieta talks people's ear off.)

Situation 2:

Cibele and Gabi get along very well. *Elas têm os mesmos gostos e <u>falam pelos cotovelos</u>.* (They have the same tastes and talk people's ear off.)

44. Por um triz

Situation 1:

Marcelo is frustrated. His soccer team suffered a 0-1 home defeat. He says to his buddy: *Por um triz eu não agarrei aquela bola.* (I was this close to catching that ball.)

Situation 2:

Seu Bernardo almost suffered an accident: He was crossing a busy street and *ele não foi atropelado por um triz* (he was two seconds from being run over by a car).

45. Briga feia

Situation 1:

Gabi is sad. *Ontem à noite, ela teve uma <u>briga feia</u> com Marcelo.* (Last night, she had a huge fight with Marcelo.)

Situation 2:

Artur: *Cara, você viu o que aconteceu depois do jogo de futebol no domingo? Teve uma <u>briga feia</u> entre os técnicos dos dois times.*

Translation:

Artur: Man, did you see what happened after the soccer game last Sunday? There was a huge fight between the two coaches.

46. Show

Situation 1:

Dona Antonieta and Seu Bernardo watched a great show de frevo in Recife.

> Dona Antonieta: *Nossa, o <u>show</u> foi maravilhoso!*

> **Translation:** Dona Antonieta: Wow, the performance was wonderful!

Frevo: Photo by Passarinho – *Prefeitura de Olinda*, Flickr, Creative Commons license

http://goo.gl/yi1hs

Cultural Note:
Recife is the capital of the state of Pernambuco and the largest metropolitan area in the North and Northeast of Brazil.

Frevo is a musical rhythm and its respective dance native to Recife. There you can watch frevo performances throughout the year and especially during the time of *Carnaval*.

Learn about the largest carnival *bloco* in the world.
Visit our blog post *Roosters in Recife Sing Frevo:*
http://goo.gl/wjw99

Situation 2:

Ana is really happy. She was given 2 tickets to see U2 in concert in São Paulo. She calls Fernando:

>*"Amor, vamos para o <u>show</u> do U2 de graça! Ganhei dois ingressos!!"*

Translation: Sweetie, we are going to U2's concert for free! I was given two tickets!!

47. Gatos pingados

Situation 1:

Last night Ana felt really sad *quando ela viu só uns <u>gatos pingados</u> na plateia de sua peça* (when she saw only a few people in the audience of her play).

Situation 2:

Cibele can't help but be happy. It's the opening of a new boutique just across the street from hers and there are not many people there. She comments:

> *"Olha lá, Gabi, só tem uns <u>gatos pingados</u> na nossa concorrente. Nossa butique é a melhor!"*

> **Translation:** Look at that, Gabi, there are only a few people at our competitor's. Our boutique is the best!

48. Ainda bem

Situation 1:

There's a storm in São Paulo and a few areas of the city had a power outage. Ana is afraid of storms and darkness. When Fernando comes home, she says:

"Ainda bem que você chegou. Estava com medo do escuro, dos relâmpagos e dos trovões."

Translation: Thank goodness you're home. I was afraid of the dark, the lightning and the thunder.

Situation 2:

Artur had some problems with his computer at work and lost all the files stored on the hard drive. *Ainda bem que ele mantém uma cópia de todos os arquivos no seu computador pessoal.* (Good thing he keeps a copy of all his files on his personal computer.)

49. Mãos à obra

Situation 1:

Fernando is thrilled. He just got the confirmation letter from his investors for the project. *Agora, mãos à obra!* (Now, let's start working!)

Situation 2:

Cibele and Gabi are discussing new decor for the boutique's display window. After they come to an agreement, Cibele says:

> "*Perfeito, nossa vitrine vai ficar linda! Mãos à obra, Gabi!*"

Translation: Perfect, our display window is going to be gorgeous! Let's get to work, Gabi!

50. Fazer questão

Situation 1:

Marcelo is sorry for what he said to Gabi. He wants to make it up to her and invites her out for dinner. She accepts the invitation and asks where they should meet.

Marcelo: *Pego você no trabalho.*

Gabi: *Não precisa. Eu encontro você no restaurante.*

Marcelo: *Eu <u>faço questão</u>.*

Translation:

Marcelo: I'll pick you up at work.

Gabi: There's no need. I'll meet you at the restaurant.

Marcelo: I insist.

Situation 2:

Ana went to Cibele's boutique and accidentally stained a dress with lipstick.

Cibele: *Não se preocupe, Ana. Nós podemos lavá-lo a seco.*

Ana: *Nada disso. <u>Faço questão</u> de pagar pelo vestido.*

Translation:

Cibele: Don't worry, Ana. We can dry clean it.

Ana: Nothing of the sort. I insist on paying for the dress.

51. Em cima do muro

Situation 1:

Dona Antonieta can't wait to meet Gabi. Marcelo has been talking about her for a while now. *Infelizmente, ele ainda está em cima do muro em relação a namorar sério com a Gabi.* (Unfortunately, he is still on the fence about seriously dating Gabi.)

Situation 2:

Cibele: *E aí, Ana, o Fernando já decidiu se vai com você para Los Angeles?*

Ana: *Nada. Ele ainda está em cima do muro.*

Translation:

Cibele: So, Ana, has Fernando decided whether he is going with you to L.A.?

Ana: Nope. He is still on the fence.

The Authors:

Luciana Lage and Renata Barboza-Murray teach Portuguese as a foreign language with Street Smart Brazil, a language and culture center dedicated to growing a community that is fully engaged in learning about Brazil and speaking Portuguese.

Luciana Lage founded Street Smart Brazil drawing on her passion for her native language and culture and based on her many years of experience teaching Portuguese. She has also taught Portuguese at the University of California, Berkeley.

Renata Barboza-Murray has been teaching both English and Portuguese as a foreign language for more than nine years. Renata has a BA in Translation (English-Portuguese) and a TESOL (Teaching English to Speakers of Other Languages) certificate.

Luciana Lage

Renata Barboza-Murray

The Company:

Street Smart Brazil offers Portuguese Classes, Intercultural Coaching, and Translation and Interpretation services by expert professionals at competitive rates. Our personalized Portuguese Classes are offered both via webcam (worldwide) and in person (San Francisco Bay Area). Choose from one-on-one lessons, group classes, and organizational training. Please visit us at StreetSmartBrazil.com

Expressions in Alphabetical Order

**Download our Flashcards
for Android**
http://goo.gl/EjC8K

Printed in Great Britain
by Amazon.co.uk, Ltd.,
Marston Gate.